WHO WOULD WIN?®

ULTIMATE JUNGLE RUMBLE

BY
JERRY PALLOTTA

ILLUSTRATED BY
ROB BOLSTER

Scholastic Inc.

16-CREATURE BRACKET

Written especially for Hugh M. Dellelo.
—J.P.
Illustrated especially for baby Breslin.
—R.B.

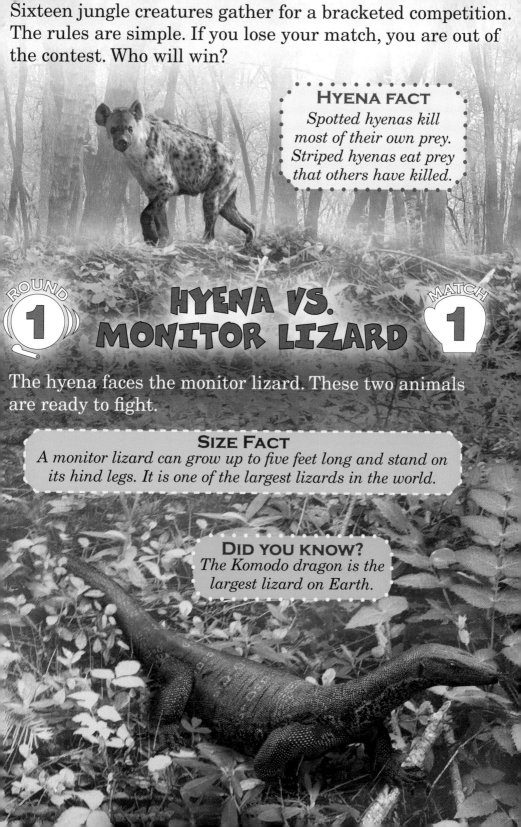

Sixteen jungle creatures gather for a bracketed competition. The rules are simple. If you lose your match, you are out of the contest. Who will win?

HYENA FACT
Spotted hyenas kill most of their own prey. Striped hyenas eat prey that others have killed.

HYENA VS. MONITOR LIZARD

The hyena faces the monitor lizard. These two animals are ready to fight.

SIZE FACT
A monitor lizard can grow up to five feet long and stand on its hind legs. It is one of the largest lizards in the world.

DID YOU KNOW?
The Komodo dragon is the largest lizard on Earth.

This fight pits a reptile against a mammal. The monitor lizard is rugged and tough, but it may be no match for the hyena.

JAW FACT
A hyena has powerful jaws that can break bones.

HYENA WINS!

The hyena knocks the lizard over and bites a chunk out of

Many gorillas have black fur. Gorillas are sociable, which means they live in families with other gorillas.

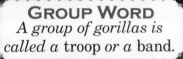

GROUP WORD
A group of gorillas is called a troop or a band.

GORILLA VS. BLACK MAMBA

The black mamba is a fast, venomous snake. It is matched against a gorilla, the largest of all apes.

COMPARE
What's the difference between venomous and poisonous? When you bite or touch an animal and get sick, that animal is poisonous. When an animal bites, stings, or stabs you, injects venom, and makes you sick, that animal is venomous.

SPEED FACT
The black mamba can slither up to twelve miles per hour.

The intelligent gorilla knows the black mamba is dangerous. The snake aims to give a fatal bite.

GORILLA WINS!

The gorilla picks up a heavy rock and drops it on the snake. The gorilla defeats the snake!

COLOR FACT
The black mamba got its name because the skin color on the inside of its mouth is black.

capybara is the largest of all rodents. Today it will fight a poison dart frog.

FEET FACT
Capybaras have webbed feet and are great swimmers.

ROUND 1
CAPYBARA VS. POISON DART FROG
MATCH 3

The frog is small, but watch out. It is poisonous! The poison dart frog is a bright color to warn other animals to stay away. Can it win this battle?

WARNING!
The skin of a poison dart frog is toxic. Don't touch it, don't eat it!

FACT
Frogs do not have claws or toenails.

The fight begins. The capybara is usually friendly with other animals. Today it has a problem. How can it win? Biting the poisonous frog would kill the capybara.

TINY FACT
Most poison dart frogs are the size of a golf ball or smaller.

CAPYBARA WINS!

The heavy capybara rolls over the frog, squishes it, and wins! The capybara's fur protects it from the frog's poisonous skin. It will move on to the second round.

A peacock in the contest? It is a show-off, not a fighter. The peacock has sharp claws. Will its colorful display of feathers help it or hinder it?

QUESTION
Is it silly to think a bird could win?

ROUND 1

PEACOCK VS. BONGO

MATCH 4

The peacock is matched against a bongo. A bongo is the largest antelope that lives in the jungle. It can weigh up to nine hundred pounds.

SMALL FACT
The smallest antelope is the royal antelope.

9

The peacock flashes its tail feathers. It stares down the bongo. The bongo is not impressed. The bongo lowers its horns and tramples the peacock.

BONGO WINS!

OTHER ANTELOPES

Other kinds of antelopes include springboks, blackbucks, impalas, gemsboks, nyalas, gazelles, and topis. Look them up!

The next matchup is a red panda against a warthog. The red panda is an herbivore, an animal that eats mostly plants. A red panda usually lives in a forest where bamboo grows.

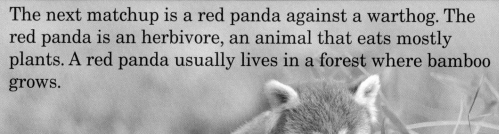

The red panda is the cutest animal in this book. It looks like a cross between a toy, a raccoon, and a house cat.

ROUND 1

RED PANDA VS. WARTHOG

MATCH 5

The warthog is an omnivore, an animal that eats everything.

The warthog and the red panda fight. The warthog has nasty teeth and is more aggressive than the red panda.

WARTHOG WINS!

SPEED FACT
Common warthogs are fast runners. They can run up to 29 mph to escape predators.

Next is a snake against a monkey. The green anaconda is one of the largest snakes in the world. The mandrill has a colorful face. It looks like it is going to a Halloween party.

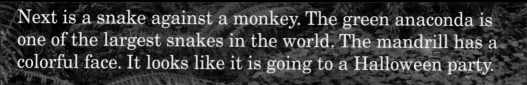

ROUND 1 GREEN ANACONDA VS. MANDRILL **MATCH 6**

The mandrill is smart. It stares at the snake. The mandrill takes the situation seriously.

FACT
Mandrills are also known as forest baboons.

The fight begins. The mandrill hopes it is strong enough to bend the snake's neck. Unfortunately, it doesn't work. The snake is too tough.

CONSTRICTOR
The anaconda is a constrictor, which means it squeezes until its prey can't breathe.

DID YOU KNOW?
One mandrill alone in the wild is unusual. In real life, a horde of mandrills might chase a snake away.

GREEN ANACONDA WINS!

The snake grabs the mandrill. The snake's many muscles work together, squeezing tighter and tighter. The snake is heading to the second round.

The leopard is one of the greatest hunters in the animal kingdom. It is sneaky, strong, and has powerful jaws and deadly claws.

FUN FACT
Leopards climb trees with ease.

NAME
Cats are also called felines.

ROUND **1**

LEOPARD VS. OKAPI

MATCH **7**

An okapi looks like part giraffe and part horse. It is a plant eater, but it can defend itself by using its huge size and kick.

FACT
An okapi is an ungulate. *Ungulates have toes on each foot, which are called* hooves.

One good kick from the okapi could break the leopard's jaw. A broken jaw would doom the leopard.

The leopard sneaks up behind the okapi. The cunning leopard avoids getting kicked. It bites the okapi's hind leg. Ouch! Now the okapi has trouble walking.

SIZE FACT
A leopard can fight, kill, and eat an animal much larger than itself.

LEOPARD WINS!

The leopard jumps on the okapi's back and bites. The okapi is losing blood. Limping and bleeding, the okapi puts up a fight but eventually loses. The leopard moves on to the

It's the last match of the first round. A giant anteater will fight a sun bear. The anteater eats insects. Its long sharp claws rip open ant mounds so the anteater can snag the ants with its long sticky tongue.

ROUND 1 — ANTEATER VS. SUN BEAR — MATCH 8

BEETLES VS. BEARS
There may be millions of different species of beetles. There are only eight types of bears.

SOME KINDS OF BEARS
Brown bear, black bear, polar bear, sun bear, grizzly bear, and spectacled bear.

The anteater's long tongue will not help in fighting the sun bear.

The sun bear walks over to the anteater and slaps its banana-shaped head. The anteater tail is long and bushy, but it can't hurt the sun bear.

The bear attacks in force, punching, biting, and stomping on the anteater. The sun bear gets a minor scratch from the anteater's claws, but that's about it. The sun bear defeats the anteater.

SUN BEAR WINS!

The eight remaining contestants move on to the second

The hyena is ready to fight the gorilla. The gorilla has a weight advantage: about four hundred pounds vs. about two hundred pounds.

LAUGH
Hyena noises sound like laughing and giggling. This animal is sometimes called a laughing hyena.

HEAD FACT
A hyena has a large neck, head, and jaws for its size.

ROUND **2** HYENA VS. GORILLA MATCH **1**

FUN FACT
A gorilla's head is larger than a human's head, but a human's brain is bigger than a gorilla's brain.

DID YOU KNOW?
Gorillas can stand or walk on two legs.

The gorilla is the stronger animal.

The hyena tries to bite the gorilla. The gorilla outmaneuvers the hyena. Like a wrestler, the gorilla puts the hyena into a headlock.

AGE FACT
Gorillas live to be about 35–45 years old.

The hyena's scary jaws are not in position to bite the gorilla. The gorilla swings its body around and uses its weight to pounce on the hyena. The hyena is in trouble.

GORILLA WINS!

The gorilla moves on to what we'll call the Jungle Four

The bongo is back after defeating the peacock. It must face the capybara, which defeated the poison dart frog.

HORN FACT

Bongo and rhinoceros horns are made of keratin, a protein that's an important part of hair and fingernails. Antlers are bone.

ROUND 2

BONGO VS. CAPYBARA

MATCH 2

The rodent must use its sharp front teeth to survive. Or it could jump in a river and out-swim the bongo. But there is no water around!

FACT

A rodent's front teeth continue to grow through its lifetime.

The bongo is thinking, "I could use my horns."

The bongo lowers its head near the ground and runs at the capybara. The capybara jumps out of the way. The bongo tries this tactic again and again. The bongo keeps o missing but the capybara is getting tired.

FACT
Horns and antlers are some of nature's best weapons.

BONGO WINS!

Eventually the bongo hits the capybara and causes damage. That's it for the big rodent! It is defeated. The bongo moves on to the next round. These jungle animals are tough!

This match features a mammal against a reptile. Legs vs. no legs. Two animals have already won their way to the Jungle Four. Now the warthog faces the green anaconda.

FACT
Warthogs have long curved tusks to fight predators.

ROUND **2**

WARTHOG VS. GREEN ANACONDA

MATCH **3**

WATER FACT
Anacondas are excellent swimmers.

The warthog is faster, and the anaconda is stronger. The warthog has sharp teeth and tusks. The snake has small teeth but a strong squeeze. Does the snake want a ham sandwich? Maybe the warthog should just run away.

Trying to decide how to defeat the snake, the warthog wanders too close. The snake uses its teeth to grab its prey and wraps itself around the warthog. Uh-oh.

BODY FACT
A green anaconda can weigh more than five hundred pounds.

DINNER FACT
After eating the warthog, the snake won't have to eat again for months.

GREEN ANACONDA WINS!

The snake slowly tightens around the warthog. Eventual.

Not many people think of the sun bear as a ferocious animal. Its favorite foods are honey and insects. The leopard is known as an excellent hunter.

WEIRD COLOR FACT
Most black panthers are leopards or jaguars with no spots.

ROUND 2

LEOPARD VS. SUN BEAR

MATCH 4

After this fight, the Jungle Four will be all set. So far we have a gorilla, bongo, and anaconda. Which animal will join them?

DID YOU KNOW?
The sun bear got its name from the marking on its chest.

The sun bear is strong and has sharp claws, but it is no match for the shifty cat. The leopard uses its paws to keep the bear off-balance.

LEOPARD WINS!

The leopard bites the bear. Repeated swipes and bites take their toll on the sun bear. The leopard moves to the third round!

26

THE JUNGLE FOUR

Round 3 has begun. Two African animals are in the same semifinal match. Fur against fur! The gorilla will fight the bongo.

DID YOU KNOW?
A gorilla does not have a tail.

 **ROUND 3**

GORILLA VS. BONGO

 MATCH 1

The two animals stare at each other. The bongo notices the gorilla's huge muscles. The gorilla sees the bongo's horns and large body.

NOWADAYS
A jungle is often called a rain forest.

This is an unusual fight. The bongo considers running away. It has no interest in the gorilla. The gorilla grabs and twists the bongo's hind leg. The gorilla is strong. It switches to the front of the bongo, grabbing its horns and twisting its front leg.

GORILLA WINS!

The bongo has trouble walking. The gorilla tips over the bongo, which crashes to the ground. The gorilla pins the bongo and wins. Who will the gorilla fight next?

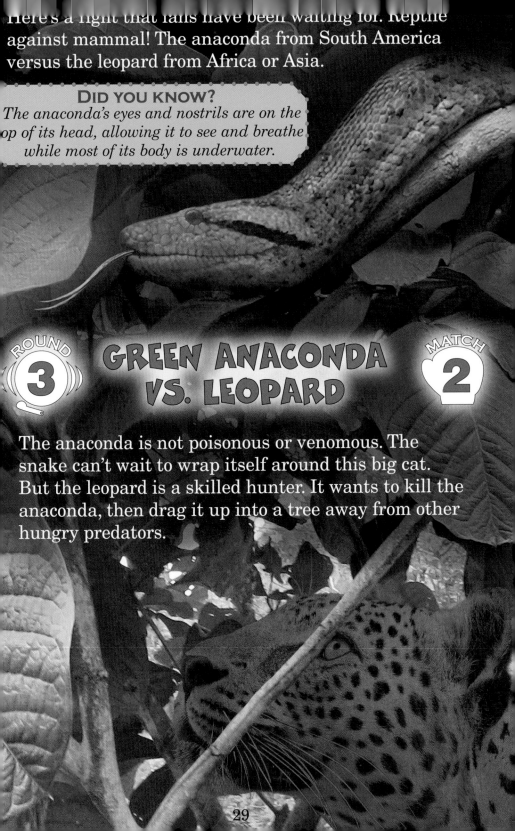

Here's a fight that fans have been waiting for. Reptile against mammal! The anaconda from South America versus the leopard from Africa or Asia.

ROUND 3

GREEN ANACONDA VS. LEOPARD

MATCH 2

The anaconda is not poisonous or venomous. The snake can't wait to wrap itself around this big cat. But the leopard is a skilled hunter. It wants to kill the anaconda, then drag it up into a tree away from other hungry predators.

The fight starts. The leopard isn't afraid to approach the snake. The leopard starts nipping and annoying the anaconda's tail end. Bite! Run! Bite! Dodge!

Whenever the snake gets close, the leopard dashes away. moves closer to the snake's midsection. The leopard has a strong jaw. Bite! Crunch! Shift away! Bite! Bite again! Ru

LEOPARD WINS!

The snake is losing blood. It no longer has the energy to encircle the leopard and try to win. The leopard goes in fo the kill. It bites the anaconda in the head. The leopard is heading to the finals. It sees the gorilla nearby!

CHAMPIONSHIP MATCH!

The leopard leaps on top of the gorilla. The gorilla uses its muscular arms to bat the leopard away. The leopard bites at the gorilla, but the gorilla grabs the smaller animal by the neck. The leopard retreats. They fight back and forth.

Four legs versus two legs and two arms. Claws versus nails. Spots versus no spots. Cat versus ape. This is the

The gorilla gets tired of fighting. But it is smart. It sees a big log and picks it up. As the leopard charges, the gorilla swings the log and smacks the leopard, breaking some bones. The big cat is in trouble.

Now the gorilla picks up a heavy rock and drops it on the wounded leopard's head. The fight is over. The gorilla wins. The gorilla may have won, but it hopes it never has to fight a giant cat again.

GORILLA WINS!

This is one way the competition might have ended. Write your own ending or think of a new version of an Ultimate Rumble book.